Contents

Foreword by Nikki Sinclaire MEP	**4 - 5**
Introduction	**6 - 9**
Section One The UK and European legislative and policy context	**11 - 17**
Section Two New directions? Coalition policy	**18 - 28**
Section Three Potential Policies	**29 - 50**
Notes	**51**

Equality in Planning

FOREWORD BY NIKKI SINCLAIRE MEP

On 30 April 2010, whilst meeting with constituents in Solihull, I received a call from a resident of Meriden. This is the charming and historic small town that proudly lays claim to be at the very geographical centre of England. In fact, this peaceful, leafy, and friendly community, with its war memorial serenely standing on its beautifully tended green, might also be seen to represent the spiritual heart of our country.

But the call I received was one of distress. A large field on the eastern edge of Meriden had been taken over by travellers, and men and machines were frantically tearing up Green Belt land – which they had legally purchased – to create hard standings and infrastructure in order to create a traveller's camp. No planning permission had been given, although an application had been handed into Solihull Council just moments before they closed for the Bank Holiday. This was to be a *fait accompli*.

But in a stunning display of community spirit, the residents rallied around, blockaded roads leading to the site, and mounted what was to become a 24 hour, 7 day a week vigil outside the camp. They were to experience intimidation from the travellers, from the police, and from the local council, but their resolve never wavered. Every legal avenue was explored and exploited; every move was watched and challenged. Jan 23 2013 marked the 1000th day of this extraordinary fight back. It was a fight for fairness, and for equality before the law. It was a fight for the Green Belt that is always under threat from planners, and which must be preserved for future generations. It was a fight for the rights of homeowners and residents to enjoy the peace and tranquillity of the community that they had all helped to build.

I have spent countless days and nights on the piquet with the good folk of Meriden, standing in the rain with a cup of coffee in my hands, and enjoying the camaraderie. I have made many trips to Solihull Council to give evidence, and have written in the press in their support. I have also made many good friends. But conflict of interests lies at the very heart of politics. Whilst the good folk of Meriden have every right to protect their legitimate interests, so the law-abiding travelling community has the right to protect its own interests.

Equality in Planning

I have become aware over the last two and a half years of failings in the system - failings that adversely affect both sides in this dispute. In areas such as healthcare and education, for example, travellers are disadvantaged. There are also failures to provide adequate space for travellers in many areas. John Prescott's ridiculous edict that effectively gives travellers 'special rights' has created resentment towards travellers amongst the settled community. If one feels marginalised, then exploiting loopholes in the planning system, and acting in opportunist self-interest may seem to be the only way forward.

Add to this mix unscrupulous property developers, attaching themselves to the travelling community and cynically using them in order to justify inappropriate and illegal development in the pursuit of profit, the abuse of Green Belt land that will anger many no matter how far away they may be from any inappropriate development, and we can see that genuine travellers and their families are caught in the middle.

Nikki Sinclaire in Meriden: Seeking solutions

My offers to meet with the travellers were sadly rejected, although I can fully understand why they might be suspicious of politicians.

But I was elected to serve all residents of the West Midlands, and so that end, I have produced this document, in which I explore possible policy options from which I hope that we can address the problems of the travellers, give reassurance and security not only to the residents of Meriden but to all, and to end the 'them and us' nature of this issue.

An Englishman's home is his castle, but I would argue that every Englishman, or woman, regardless of their lifestyle should have the chance to acquire a home, and that all communities should be able to live side by side without fear or suspicion. Laws should not merely be respected, but they must be worthy of the respect of all. At the time of writing, this is clearly not the case. Let us fix it.

NIKKI SINCLAIRE MEP

Equality in Planning

> **A fresh look at unlawful development and a 'new deal' for travellers, settled communities and the environment**

INTRODUCTION

This document is intended to stimulate discussion of the problems confronting the UK's travelling communities and the 'settled communities' who are often compelled against their will to accommodate them. Local politicians, Councils, The Planning Inspectorate and Courts often seem to assume the role of Pontius Pilate taking controversial decisions which pleases no one, undermines the sanctity of the green belt and countryside through untenable temporary permissions and – in effect – worsens the problem.

There must be a better way to promote and balance the accommodation rights of travellers with the needs and interests of the settled community and the countryside.

This document explores and outlines a range of 'potential policies' – some highly controversial – aimed at addressing both the perception and the reality of unfairness in the planning system as it affects both the travelling and the settled communities. It focuses on the twin issues of planning for Traveller sites and dealing with unauthorised developments.

There is currently grave discontent on all sides. Battle-lines are drawn up. Views are polarised and entrenched. The big guns of the political parties and vested interests are primed to boom and roar at 'prejudice' and 'unmet needs' on one side and of 'land grabs' and 'exploitation' on the other.

This is an exploration of the disputed territory. In venturing into what has been widely perceived as 'no man's land', it aims to inspire others to seek solutions. The 'potential policies' outlined in Section III are just a starting point for discussion of some of the most controversial aspects of Gypsy and Traveller provision.

Conflict has proved, as ever, destructive. Casualties and outrages increase resentment and so make ultimate resolution harder and harder. Residents are accused of being 'nimby' or worst still racist while travellers are seen as opportunistic developers openly flouting planning norms using 'human rights arguments and 'unmet need' objections' to generate the 'very special circumstances' required to overcome green belt and countryside protections.

Put simply the pro-traveller faction is deemed 'anti-resident' or even 'bleeding heart' and residents portrayed as intolerant or racist even when they have legitimate concerns. Both sides claim victim status.

Equality in Planning

This document seeks to put the challenges and issues surrounding the need for more traveller accommodation provision on the table. It aims to discuss options and outline possible solutions. More importantly, it calls on community leaders (in the settled and traveller communities), politicians and planners to come together around a new consensus for action. Leadership is not a role that can be shirked. Nationally, regionally and locally a job needs to be done to ensure appropriate plan led provision for travellers whilst discouraging destructive unlawful developments. The classic 'bank holiday blitz development' (and its many variants) undermines the reputation of travellers everywhere, destroys our valuable countryside, cost taxpayers dearly and fuels a festering sea of resentment between communities.

All such responses serve only to fuel negative stereotyping, wreck valuable ecology (and archaeology), drain scant taxpayer resources and create years of uncertainty for groups locked in an ever escalating cycle of litigation, enforcement and appeal upon appeal which often proceed at a glacial pace – further undermining the planning process.

Partisan pundits who simply want to continue to promulgate the arguments of one side should back off. Throughout this document, we will take it as a core premise that travellers and settled residents have the same freedom as anyone else to live as they will, provided that they do not violate the freedoms of others.

Inevitably, the choice of a travelling life entails inconveniences and inherent disadvantages. It is no part of the function of law or State to remove these, though it is their role to enable – which is to say, to remove hindrances to - the enjoyment of this, as any other individual freedom assured *de jure*.

By the same token, settled residents have the right to enjoy peaceful and untroubled lives, protected from violations of privacy or property. Again, the State does not provide special amenities, protect views or select neighbours. It does, however, defend the countryside and preserve the freedoms and safety of its inhabitants.

There is no point in discussing this problem until first we clear the decks of preconceptions and prejudice. The travelling community as a whole does not seek to abuse the law in order to feed on its settled hosts. The few 'parasites' - who seek to 'steal a march on the planning process and develop for greed rather than need - do enormous damage to their fellows by inspiring fear and mistrust. In fact, it is as wrong to generalise about 'the travelling community' as about, say, 'blacks' or 'aliens'. As in any such grouping, there is no doubt a small number of anti-social individuals, a number of reckless scapegraces, but there is a large majority of people anxious merely to live and to raise their families in peace according to their traditions.

Equality in Planning

The settled community in general is not opposed to travellers but it too is wary. If the relationship between the two lifestyles is to become symbiotic and mutually beneficial, we must weed out prejudice and intolerance no less than greed posing as 'need'.

The media have been particularly irresponsible in this regard, portraying individual anti-social acts as characteristic and 'travellers' as a homogenous group. On the contrary, travellers' failure to unite and make common cause has served them ill. There is little communication between its many sectors.

This is a serious attempt to identify travellers' accommodation needs and the freedoms which settled residents must enjoy and to find a means whereby these can be reconciled in justice.

One of the principal issue which 'dare not speak its name' today is that of developers from (or claiming association with) the travelling community who set out deliberately and cynically to manipulate the planning system in order to achieve inflated land values.

To cite just one example at the centre of an unlawful development dispute, one traveller sold to another a three acre plot of land valued at £15,000- £30,000. The buyer then attempted to sell the land to a reluctant settled community for some £200,000. This appears to be a clear bid to extort money from the local community and to profit from the misfortunes of others.

There are a small number of published cases where this has occurred, but there are other, lower-profile incidents which have been informally reported. Such people are Travellers' worst enemies. They fuel prejudice and so intensify the conflict.

There also appears to be a 'cosy collusion' of politicians of all parties who would prefer NOT to promote appropriately located traveller provision because it is widely perceived to be electorally unpopular. They prefer to be seen to oppose such applications, knowing that Planning Inspectors will then make the decisions for them without affecting their popularity.

One leading traveller engaged in a dispute with a Council which has established no new sites for 40 years told us, 'We have offered to swap our disputed land for any other suitable site. The Council officials want a solution. Councillors, however, want to be re-elected, and, because we are the devil incarnate in the media, establishment of a new site will always cause uproar. We've actually done them a favour by developing land without planning permission. It makes us the villains. It's much easier to be seen nominally to disapprove of us and to do nothing than to do something about it and risk losing votes.'

It has become a default practice to opt out of difficult decisions – allowing instead unelected, unconnected 'experts' to resolve complex issues. This is poor governance and the very opposite of localism. Again, by evading the responsibility to lead, they make the problem worse.

There is plenty to suggest, then, that all is not well with the systems, processes policies and frameworks whereby appropriate, needs-based provision can be made for travellers.

It need not be this way.

This document argues that nothing less than a total transformation – in thinking, policy and practice - is required to achieve appropriate traveller provision which is:

- Plan-led

- Engages all affected communities, politicians and planners

- Acknowledges and addresses the disadvantages facing the travelling community (health, economic, education, discrimination etc).

- Dispels myths and preconceptions and restores reputations

- Protects valued environments

- Fosters trust and mutual respect

- Promotes social cohesion and sustainability

- Prevents abuse of the Planning Process

- Gives Local Authorities new tools to grapple with the issue – prevention as well as enforcement

- Embraces the wider issues relating to this issue (e.g. legal) and suggests reform

- Seeks equitable solutions

Although the Government has pledged new money for traveller provision, this must be accompanied by brand new thinking to address the failings of the current system. We believe that the proposed changes in Planning Policy and imminent new Ministerial Guidelines will not give Gypsies, Travellers, Politicians, Planners and the settled community the tools required to attain these ends.

Equality in Planning

SECTION I summarises the UK and European policy and the historical and legislative context in which decisions relevant to traveller provision must be made.

SECTION II looks at new policy directions as referred to in the Coalitions 'Planning for Traveller Sites' document.

SECTION III looks at no fewer than 17 **potential policy suggestions** derived from a range of sources and – perhaps most fittingly – from communities who have been most affected by inappropriate and often unlawful development. It is not suggested that all mooted policies should be pursued by any Government or Council but that those responsible for policy in this area should carefully consider their merits and applicability to replace or complement current policies.

The 'next steps' section is for individuals, groups and political parties to take up the issue and communicate their views directly to their own Government, Local Planning Authority, Parish Council or representative. Comments can also be made to the email address provided within this document.

Equality in Planning

SECTION I

The UK and European legislative and policy context

Definition:

For the purposes of this discussion document, "gypsies and travellers" means:

Persons of nomadic habit of life, whatever their race or origin, including such persons who, on grounds only of their own or their family's or dependants' educational or health needs or old age, have ceased to travel temporarily or permanently, but excluding members of an organised group of travelling show people or circus people travelling together as such.

This is a widely used and broadly satisfactory definition. Although we accept this definition throughout the document, we presume to discuss in the next section a 'duty of proof' which should be applied to individuals who claim to have a nomadic – or recently ceased nomadic - lifestyle, and who (for the purposes of a planning application) have a consequent land requirement relevant to that need.

A brief historical overview:

In the immediate post-war period, there was unprecedented urban development in the UK. Many long-established stopping places were developed and converted to housing estates etc. **The Caravan Sites and Control of Development Act 1960** also closed common land to Gypsies and Travellers.

These measures created an unquestionable shortage of appropriate sites which has, in many areas, endured to this day. Gypsies and Travellers were often compelled to camp ad hoc on tracts of land deemed by some to be inappropriate, so causing unparalleled tension between communities. Agrarian labour, a mainstay of the nomadic economy and the principal means of integration, dried up, replaced by mechanisation. As the gypsy population regenerated after the porajmos (the Nazi 'devouring' during which approximately 200,000 and 500,00 Gypsies were murdered during World War 2) , the issue of accommodation need grew still more pressing.

In a bid to ease it, **The 1968 Caravan Sites Act** created a duty on local authorities to establish sites for Travellers.

Equality in Planning

The Criminal Justice and Public Order Act of 1994, however, repealed the 1968 act and scrapped that obligation on Councils, replacing it with **Planning Circular 1/94**. This well-meaning but mealy-mouthed provision requested that Councils should help travellers to identify land suitable for purchase and development as travellers' sites. Only if no such sites could be found were other criteria to be applied.

In theory, then, this was an intelligent bid to solve the problem by co-operation between travellers and the settled communities as represented by their Councils. In practice, most authorities, no doubt dreading the disapproval of settled communities failed to find any such sites, leaving it rather to travellers to identify suitable land then rejecting their applications on the basis of theoretical criteria.

Overall, then, post-war developments, lack of political will and bad law created a shortage of approved sites for bona fide travellers. In 2004, The Office of the Deputy Prime Minister estimated that over 3,500 Gypsies and travellers had no legal place where they could stay. They were therefore defined under the Housing Act 1996 as homeless.

This situation set the scene for further unmet need accompanied by unlawful development, further rises in community tension, protracted legal and planning disputes and a fracture in the possibility of peaceful co-existence between growing sections of the travelling and settled communities.

The legal and policy context – clearly influenced by European Union Directives - is as follows:

- **The Race Relations Act 1976** makes it unlawful to treat someone less favourably on the grounds of colour, race, nationality, ethnic or national origins. **The Race Relations Amendment Act and Regulation of 2000 and 2003** respectively, transposed the EU Race Equality Directive into British law.

  These acts state that **Romany Gypsies** and **Irish Travellers** are defined in law as racial groups and are thereby protected by British anti-discrimination legislation. This legislation also extends the responsibilities of local authorities to promote equality of opportunity.

- **The Human Rights Act 1998** also protects Gypsies and Travellers from discrimination. It gives further legal effect in the UK to the fundamental rights and freedoms contained in the European Convention on Human Rights (in particular **Article 8** 'Right to private and family life')

Equality in Planning

This Act should form part of a local authority's decision-making with regards to Gypsies and Travellers. **Draft Planning Circular (54)** states 'The provisions of the European Convention on Human Rights should be considered as an integral part of local authorities' decision making... Local planning authorities should consider the consequences of refusing or granting planning permission, or taking enforcement action, on the rights of the individuals concerned - both Gypsies and Travellers and local Residents - and whether it is necessary and proportionate in the circumstances.'

Proportionality may mean that a local authority may decide to suspend an eviction or find an alternative site because of the human cost in terms of trauma, homelessness, poor access to services, financial factors etc.

Article 8 of the Act is associated with some Traveller cases. 'Everyone has the right to respect for his private and family life [and] his home…and there should be no interference by a public authority with the exercise of this right except such as is in accordance with the law and is necessary in a democratic society in the interests of national security, public safety or the economic well-being of the country, for the prevention of disorder or crime, for the protection of health or morals, or for the protection of the rights and freedoms of others.'

Article 8 therefore has to be balanced out with the needs of the wider community as well as the interests of Gypsies and Travellers. It cannot be seen as constituting an unchecked basis for Gypsies and Travellers to establish encampments without fear of legal sanction. On the contrary, it outlines with equal force the rights of the nomadic and the settled, which may often conflict.

In the case of **Sally Chapman** VS the United Kingdom, the claimant, went to the European Court of Human Rights because a local authority refused her application to live on land she owned. The court decided that the council *had* interfered with the rights of her family (article 8) but that these actions were justified because of the need to protect the rights of the wider community and to preserve the environment.

Specifically The Court held that Article 8 implied positive state obligations to facilitate the Gypsy way of life. However it applied the exception of Article 8 that the interference was "necessary in a democratic society", since the land inhabited by the Gypsy family was the subject of environmental protection and therefore a wide margin of discretion was to be accorded to national authorities in planning issues.

Equality in Planning

- **Use of the European Court of Human Rights for Planning Appeal purposes.**
  There has been just one case in Britain (**Chichester v Doe & Others**) where a council (Stroud) approved a site because it believed that it was obliged to do so under human rights law. This was widely reported in the press as an HRA case which would mean that local authorities could not deal with unauthorised developments.

  In fact, this case involved Gypsies on land with no special designation. The inspector, furthermore, concluded that there was minimal visual impact. The Court of Appeal upheld the inspector's reasoning on the grounds that Chichester had consistently failed to permit Travellers' sites in the area despite proven need and so was in breach of Article 8. This is an important judgement, but the circumstances were peculiar and specific. Chichester v Doe can be regarded as a precedent only in rare cases.

  It is also worth mentioning a much cited but oft misunderstood case which relates to the HRA & Traveller provision - **'the Connors case'** (Connors v. the United Kingdom). The European Court of Human Rights found that the summary eviction of applicants from a Gypsy site without reasoned justification or sufficient procedural safeguards breached the right to respect for private life and the home under Article 8. **This is the only case where Travellers won a case in the ECHR and it involved a local authority site where the Travellers paid rent. It was not a planning case.**

- **The Equalities Act 2010** states that: 'A public authority must, in the exercise of its functions, have due regard to the need to advance equality of opportunity between persons who share a relevant protected characteristic and persons who do not share it… [As well as] encourage persons who share a relevant protected characteristic to participate in public life or in any other activity in which participation by such persons is disproportionately low.' Gypsies and Travellers are recognised as having a protected characteristic under this Act. Case law has also established that the Government has a duty to *"facilitate the gypsy way of life"* for ethnic Gypsies and Travellers under the Human Rights Act.

- **The Housing Act 2004** imposes a duty on local district housing authorities to provide appropriate accommodation for Gypsies and Travellers. This duty means that authorities must assess the accommodation needs of Gypsies and Travellers and include a strategy to meet those needs within their wider housing strategies.

Equality in Planning

- **Ministerial guidance (Planning Circulars)** A Circular, which has for a number of years played an important part in guiding Local Authority and Planning Inspectorate decisions, has recently been revoked. It is worth mentioning as part of background context. **Circular 01/2006:** *Planning for Gypsy and Traveller Caravan Sites,* which the Government has described as 'flawed' because it states that new sites in the Green Belt are "normally inappropriate development "as defined in **Planning Policy Guidance 2: Green Belts (now defunct).** The inclusion of the word "normally" gives rise to applications by travellers whose exceptional or 'abnormal' status can be claimed to justify more favourable treatment than applications from members of the settled community. Data from the Planning Inspectorate suggests that, between 2006 and 2009, 60 per cent of planning appeals for traveller development in the Green Belt were allowed. **This is compared to just 19 per cent over the same period for minor housing appeals (i.e. 10 homes or less).**

- Circular 01/06 has generated a new legacy of unsustainable 'temporary permissions' which need to be addressed. Temporary permissions do not provide the security of tenure/occupation sought by the applicants nor – in the main – the environmental outcomes sought by the Council and local residents e.g. the standard of landscaping expected in respect of a permanent permission, for example, may not be able to be imposed.

- In addition, circular 01/06 views sustainability in ambiguous terms, implying that owing to the type of vehicles used by Gypsies and Travelers' (4 x 4, lorries, trailers, caravans, scrap vehicles etc.) exceptions should be made for this. In the context of a temporary permission, this could be disastrous for the countryside (or green belt) in which the site is located. Larger volumes of very large vehicles will have detrimental effects on verges, road surfaces and local wildlife and pose an exponentially great potential for vehicular conflict with other road users, walkers, horse riders etc.

- It is not unusual for planning inspectors on appeal to grant a temporary permission whilst at the same time observing that the appeal site is situated at a generally unsustainable location. Obviously, once families have established themselves on these sites, relocation will raise substantial problems.

- Even when temporary permissions become 'permanent' many sites fail the test of sustainability undermining the health and wellbeing of occupants. We shall return to this theme below.

Equality in Planning

- **Circular 04/2007:** *Planning for Travelling Showpeople.* Circulars 01/2006. This circular in effected replicated much of the 01/06 circular but was aimed at specifically promoting sites for travelling show people 'who do not in general share the same culture or traditions as Gypsies and Travellers'. Such sites would be for mixed residential and business use, to enable the effective storage and repair of significant amounts of equipment. Issues relevant travelling show people are not the focus of this document.

- **European Union Directives:** Member States are already under an obligation to give Roma (like other EU citizens) non-discriminatory access to education, employment, vocational training, healthcare, social protection and housing through Directive 2000/43/EC.

- **'An EU Framework for National Roma Integration Strategies up to 2020'** The European anti-discrimination and pro-social integration influence on British policy and legislation (relating to Roma) is set to continue principally through this strategy aimed at the 10-12 million estimated Roma population living within EU member states. Action is current and new policy is expected:

    'Member States are requested to prepare or revise their national Roma integration strategies and present them to the Commission by the end of December 2011. In spring 2012, ahead of the annual Roma Platform meeting, the Commission will assess these national strategies and report to the European Parliament and to the Council about progress.

This 'request' however makes it clear that the European Union recognises that a tailored approach is required within each Country and that the EU should not be prescriptive in 'how' this should be dealt with across its entire territories.

   'whilst Roma constitute Europe's largest minority, the size of the Roma community as a percentage of the total population in each Member State varies significantly, and the scale of the challenges which Member States face, as well as their starting points for tackling Roma exclusion, are likely to differ in magnitude...

   'We do not expect the Communication to change the Government's existing policies and approaches to identifying and reducing inequalities, for example, amongst the Gypsy and Traveller communities in the UK, and we are content to clear the document from scrutiny. However, in light of the differences in the situation of Roma across

the EU, we agree with the Government that any Council Conclusions based on the Communication should not be prescriptive as to the form or content of national Roma integration strategies and that any EU monitoring mechanism should be proportionate to the challenges confronting different Member States...'

This, then, is the background against which new legislation will be framed and new initiatives launched, to ensure that the valid concerns of travellers and settled communities are taken into consideration and effectively addressed.

Compromise will always be needed. Prejudice against the travelling community is deep-seated and dates back over a millennium and more. The redtop Press, seizing upon every genuine crime and misdemeanour but also quick to propagate myth, has fostered fear in the general public. Resultant resentment and mistrust on the part of Travellers and the settled communities have hardened into mutual suspicion regarding almost any traveller development activity:

Equality in Planning

SECTION TWO

New directions? Coalition policy

The current view of the coalition executive's policy (for England only) can be found in the New Ministerial guidance (*Planning Policy for Traveller Sites*), published in March 2012.

The stated rationale for the introduction of a new Planning Circular was stated in the preceding consultation document:

> *'Many people think that current planning policy treats traveller sites more favourably than it does other housing and that it is easier for one group of people to gain planning permission, particularly on Green Belt land. This has led people to believe that the system is unfair. The Government believes that by being fair to both the traveller and the settled communities, people are more likely to get on together.*

a view with which we heartily concur.

The over-arching purpose of the new Circular is:

to ensure fair and equal treatment for travellers, in a way that facilitates the traditional and nomadic way of life of travellers while respecting the interests of the settled community.

The stated aims of the new circular in respect of traveller sites are:

- that local planning authorities should make their own assessment of need for the purposes of planning

- to ensure that local planning authorities, working collaboratively, develop fair and effective strategies to meet need through the identification of land for sites

- to encourage local planning authorities to plan for sites over a reasonable timescale

- that plan-making and decision-taking should protect Green Belt from inappropriate development

- to promote more private traveller site provision while recognising that there will always be those travellers who cannot provide their own sites

- that plan-making and decision-taking should aim to reduce the number of unauthorised developments and encampments and make enforcement more effective

Equality in Planning

- for local planning authorities to ensure that their Local Plan includes fair, realistic and inclusive policies

- to increase the number of traveller sites in appropriate locations with planning permission, to address under provision and maintain an appropriate level of supply

- to reduce tensions between settled and traveller communities in plan-making and planning decisions

- to enable provision of suitable accommodation from which travellers can access education, health, welfare and employment infrastructure

- for local planning authorities to have due regard to the protection of local amenity and local environment.

These aims are without exception desirable and should be supported.

As it stands, however, the document begs a number of questions.

It is worth exploring whether the provisions outlined in the circular can provide justice and assurance to the travelling and the settled communities alike, with particular regard to householders' security from 'invasion' and the improvement of Travellers' life-prospects? It is also worth exploring the areas still uncharted and look further forward to expected and (and other) changes that could still yet be made.

The context needs stressing too: At present, 'Gypsies and Travellers are 12 percent more likely to have a long-term illness than comparable members of the settled community... mothers are 20 times more likely to experience the death of a child than the rest of the population... and school attendance and educational attainment of Gypsy and Traveller pupils have been considerably lower than their peers at every key stage...'

To deal with these issues we pose a number of key questions and suggest responses.

(a) Should the current definitions of Gypsies, Travellers be re-visited as it relates to Planning issues?

This definition is derived from case law. It is difficult to envisage another which does not require extensive investigation of ancestry, culture etc. The current definition avoids unnecessary time-wasting at appeals where it is obvious that an applicant has (had) a nomadic lifestyle and extensive local gypsy family connections.

Equality in Planning

The only problem is that the current definition requires people to have a nomadic habit of life unless they have ceased to travel for educational or health needs or old age. In the context of a planning application it can be very difficult for an authority to gather evidence on travelling habits and whether these amount to 'a nomadic habit of life'.

Reasons for having ceased to travel may also be difficult to verify. Such enquiries cause needless dispute and create an unnecessary burden on local planning authorities.

We therefore recommend that the definition itself carries an additional provision stating: *'where applicants wish to establish a Gypsy or Traveller site, they must submit evidence of their traveller lifestyle, including current or previous nomadic habit, and/or reasons for cessation. Evidence should be capable of verification. The 'burden of proof' should lie with the applicants - not the Local Planning Authority.'*

(b) **Where need has been identified, should local planning authorities set targets for the provision of sites in their local planning policies against which Planning decisions and subsequent appeals will – in all circumstances - be made?**

The current circular requires Local Authorities to:

a. identify and update annually, a supply of specific deliverable sites sufficient to provide five years' worth of sites against their locally set targets

b. identify a supply of specific, developable sites or broad locations for growth, for years six to ten and, where possible, for years 11-15 "

> Strict numerical targets in general diminish responsiveness and give rise to inappropriate decisions. Declared targets, however, not only motivate but reassure the several concerned communities that their needs are being addressed. Demand for sites is frequently variable, unpredictable or not easily quantifiable. In all such cases, targets should be *indicative* as distinct from imperative in order to ensure flexibility and responsiveness to increased or decreased need. There should be no requirement, however, that sites be allocated in a Local Development Plan sufficient to meet a target, since targets may be achieved or exceeded piecemeal over time as planning applications come forward and suitable sites become available.

Equality in Planning

In addition, Local authorities may not be able to choose from a wide range of areas proposed (in fact it may be that very few sites will be brought forward despite calls for them). Almost any proposed site could prove controversial. Landowners and property owners at or near such sites will be concerned about the effects of 'blight' once such locations are disclosed. Even the suggestion that land might be so used can cause uproar.

As an aside, we welcome the removal in this draft PPS of any reference to the *need* to consider such areas and to compulsory purchase within a specific time. The implication is that only sites which come forward from willing landowners should be considered. Such sites would – as with any residential development – be subject to lengthy debate and feasibility studies which might well probably render impracticable a five year plan with local consent.

Monitoring a five year supply requires considerable work - gathering evidence of completions and forecasts of future building rates for an annual monitoring report. During a period of financial austerity, this is work that could be removed from the local planning authority, thereby freeing officers to deal with specific applications.

There is also no guarantee that the sites identified by officers accord with the requirements of prospective Traveller-developers. Monitoring of indicative targets could be undertaken in relation to the target without the detail required for a five year supply to be evidenced.

Although conspicuous and consistent failure to meet them should be regarded as a failure, targets should not be so imperative as to outweigh practical considerations, nor should resident taxpayers pay the price of local authorities' incompetence.

(c) **Should local planning authorities plan for local need in the context of historical demand?**

Historical demand may be an important indicator but is not necessarily an accurate guide to future trends in Gypsy and Traveller site needs. Local Authorities need to be able to react to events which have little to do with local historical demand e.g. displacement from unauthorised sites in surrounding areas, expiry of temporary permission at neighbouring sites, inward migration which has not hitherto been evident etc. Local Authorities should therefore be able to plan flexibly for site need based on 'robust evidence' of current need and by the use of other relevant intelligence which indicates future need (be it short or medium term).

Equality in Planning

Local Authorities also have to consider the 'type' of 'demand' evident in a specific area. The fact of an occasional roadside encampment at a specific site in the past, for example, is not sufficient warrant to assert an historic need for a permanent site.

(d) **How far does the new circular actually protect Green Belts and other specially designated sites (e.g. Areas of Outstanding Natural Beauty, Sites of Special Scientific Interest, Local Wildlife sites)?**

The phrase 'normally inappropriate' was removed from the previous circular (which allowed traveller developers to cite a range of reasons why although such development would normally be inappropriate there was a range reasons why such inappropriateness could now be overcome).

Although this 'loophole' may have been closed there are two circumstances in which traveller developers will still seek to overcome protections to countryside sites which apply to the settled communities.

(1) The new circular states:

if a local planning authority cannot demonstrate an up–to-date five-year supply of deliverable sites, this should be a significant material consideration in any subsequent planning decision when considering applications for the grant of temporary planning permission

It could be argued therefore that the 'door is still wide open' for traveller developers to launch 'temporary' applications for developments (unlawful or otherwise) at inappropriate locations with some prospect of success.

Although this Circular and a related circular (11/95) seeks to reassure that 'There is no presumption that a temporary planning permission should become permanent' it is clearly the practice amongst many authorities to 'legitimise' temporary sites over time where resident opposition has subsided and the unmet need targets are pursued. This practice militates against plan led policies as temporary sites can still be inappropriately located failing many of the tests of 'sustainability'. The imperative to provide an up to date five year supply by March 2013 (when the provisions of the new circular comes into effect) is likely to give fresh impetus to this practice. The consequences of this will continue to feed negative views of travellers and the planning process and will be at the expensive of (otherwise) protected countryside sites and traveller relations with the wider community.

Equality in Planning

The principles underpinning planning policies should apply across the board. There are many deprived and deserving people in the settled community (not to mention the homeless) to whom no such concessions are made. Nothing so engenders resentment and fuels age-old prejudices as the claiming – and, still worse, the granting – of exemptions from restraints experienced by the general public.

At present, many settled communities see Traveller sites approved in large measure only because they have been established without official approval and have hitherto been reluctantly tolerated. Enforced habituation spares planners and elected legislators the initial furore whilst fulfilling rigid targets set by distant, unaccountable regional bodies. This is planning by force majeure – also known as 'bullying'. In bending rules in favour of a sectional interest rather than the public good, it militates against good relations between communities and ignores the true purpose of Planning, which is to monitor and control land-use in the public interest.

The settled community is alienated by 'normally inappropriate' sites unlawfully developed by Travellers and only retrospectively approved on appeal even though residents and the local authority have signalled their objections.

Unauthorised 'Bank Holiday developments' in particular are clear attempts by Traveller-developers to 'steal a march' on the planning process and to establish a *fait accompli* whilst Council offices are closed. Where this activity is rewarded by approval – retrospectively or at appeal – this is seen as institutionalised bias in the planning system which ignores the human rights and views of the settled population and as an abnegation of duty on the part of their elected leaders.

These situations should not arise. Only co-operation between landlords, travellers and local authorities, pro-actively seeking sites and working with the local community will see sites established peaceably and in the best interests of all parties.

Decisions should be made on the intrinsic merits of planning applications. There should be no suggestion that temporary applications should be 'considered favourably'. Such a phrase could be seen to be providing travellers with special rights in a similar way to Circular 01/2006 which states that 'substantial weight' should be given to unmet need when considering temporary permission.

Equality in Planning

Arguably, the proposed wording will to result in more permissions than the original Circular. The inclusion of this phrase is not considered to be consistent with Planning Policy Statement 3 on Housing. There is nothing in that PPS relating to temporary permissions in this context, and all consideration of housing applications is done in the context of all the relevant policies.

Suggesting that there will be situations where temporary applications will, in effect, be approved even if they are unsatisfactory will maintain the 'widespread perception that the system is unfair and that it is easier for one group of people to gain planning permission' referred to in the Ministerial foreword to this draft PPS.

It is therefore more realistic for LPA's to have further to both assess potential need and make suitable provision against the authorities own 'robust evidenced based criteria

Local authorities should not feel compelled to renew temporary permissions simply because there are no alternatives. A longer transitional period should be used by both travellers and the local authority to identify more suitable sites - particularly when these sites are at sites where they are a source of considerable community tension.

 (e) **What other measures are being announced by the Government in respect of unlawful traveller developments?**

On the 21st of December 2012 the Government launched a new consultation document which focuses on changes to a specific enforcement device i.e. a Temporary Stop Notice (TSN).

The consultation document: 'Changes to Temporary Stop Notices: revoking Statutory Instrument 2005/206' has far reaching consequences for occupants of caravans involved in unlawful development.

The scope of the consultation document succinctly outlines the rationale, impact and checks and balances involved in the proposed changes:

Equality in Planning

SCOPE OF THIS CONSULTATION

A local council can issue a Temporary Stop Notice if they think that there has been a breach of planning control and that it is expedient that the activity is stopped immediately. Temporary Stop Notices apply for 28 days, during which the local council is able to assess the circumstances and determine whether to take further enforcement action. In most cases regulations prevent Temporary Stop Notices being used to prohibit the stationing of caravans used as main residences (the exception being where the local council considers that the resulting risk of harm to the public interest is so serious as to outweigh any benefit to the occupier of the caravan).

Intentional unauthorised development undermines confidence in the planning system. The Government wants to see fair play in planning: cutting unnecessary red tape and bureaucracy, whilst ensuring that the rules and protections which do remain are applied equally, fairly, and with due process.

As regulations currently limit the circumstances in which local councils can use Temporary Stop Notices in respect of caravans used as main residences, this may discourage or prohibit their use in some instances where they could be beneficial.

The availability of appropriate alternative sites for caravans used as main residences will be a factor in determining whether it would be appropriate to use Temporary Stop Notices to stop such unauthorised development (i.e. if there is suitable site provision to which the unauthorised caravans could be relocated). Revoking Statutory Instrument 2005/206 to give councils greater freedom to determine whether to use Temporary Stop Notices.

Equality in Planning

So, currently TSN's have the effect of stopping unlawful development but do not stop unlawful occupation. In Meriden (for example) the unlawful development was stopped by a Temporary Stop Notice (and further development stopped by other devices such as use of Injunction thereafter) but NO powers existed to compel the occupants to cease occupation. Some of the occupants therefore continued to live in an uncompleted 'quagmire' of a development for some three years while the planning and appeals process was traversed.

Under these proposed changes a Council would be able to stop occupation (a) if there are other (lawful) sites to relocate caravan occupants to and (b) where Councils are confident that they are not breaching the human rights of the occupants. In the Meriden case it is highly unlikely that a TSN which stopped occupation of the caravans would have been implemented as the Council had 'unmet need' (in terms of traveller sites) and the travellers refused to declare themselves homeless (which would have rendered them liable to 'bricks and mortar' relocation.

Meriden residents protest outside the ECHR, Strasbourg with Nikki Sinclaire MEP

This would continue to be unsatisfactory to all parties:

- Residents would continue to feel that unlawful development/ occupation is being tolerated
- Travellers would continue to reside at an unsuitable site
- The (Greenbelt/Local Wildlife Site) environment would continue to suffer and
- No quick remedy is in site as the glacial pace of the decision/appeal spiral works its way forward over a number of years

HOWEVER

The rationale of the revised TSN is that a Meriden (type) situation COULD be averted if Councils have a surplus of traveller pitches (e.g. unused and available pitches locally) at appropriate / approved locations. In such situations TSN's could be deployed against unlawfully located caravans in the knowledge that viable relocation options ARE available.

So the key (again) for LPA's to be able to use this tool of enforcement is where they are committed to (and providing) against unmet need.

It is worth noting the Governments' comments on the impact of unlawfully located caravans:

Equality in Planning

The potential detrimental impacts of caravans being moved onto land and used as main residences will generally be greater than a change of use to an existing building which is already part of the landscape. With buildings there is also an opportunity for the local council to take enforcement action during the construction process, whereas this would not be possible in relation to caravans.

As with the current TSN there is no instant appeal available to traveller developers. This is desirable as TSN's are – as of necessity – designed to halt unlawful developments which are causing or pose a serious threat to (e.g.) the environment, community, developers, site occupants. Councils need to be (a) clear as to why they are implementing a TSN (b) confident that they are no contravening the human rights of developers/ occupants and (c) Have other sites to available to relocate unlawful dwellers. Developers retain the right of judicial review which is an appropriate 'check' on a TSN

The timescale for consultation to be concluded is February the 13th 2013. Prior to the publication of the final version of the new TSN's the Government needs to make clear (possibly through guidance) the answer to a number of key questions

We have listed TEN KEY QUESTIONS which need to be addressed to enable an assessment as to the role that a new TSN could play in preventing and addressing unlawful developments. These are:

1/ Does the Government envisage a 'Gretna Green Effect' whereby unlawful caravans would simply move across the English border into Wales or Scotland where the revised TSN's do not apply? Does the Government have information as to whether Wales and Scotland are likely to 'harmonise' on this issue to prevent this effect?

2/ Will the Government issue guidance for Councils so that they can be confident that they are deploying the new TSN's without breaching Equalities Legislation or the Human Rights/ 'protected characteristics' of travellers.'

Romany Gypsies and Irish Travellers are racial groups, which share protected characteristics under equalities law'

3/ Where a Council has (a) met its assessed need (against a robust evidence base) but (b) is still faced with unlawful traveller developments (e.g. from other areas) and (c) has no available local provision can it STILL use TSN's to relocate caravans to other areas (in agreement with other Councils under the 'duty to co-operate)

4/ Emphasis is focused on caravans used in 'respect of caravans used as main residences'. Does the new TSN's include other caravans and temporary structures located unlawfully (e.g. empty caravans, sheds, Lorries, Plant and equipment left idle)

Equality in Planning

5/ Does the Government anticipate a 'targeting' effect i.e. would unauthorised traveller developers target Local Authority areas where (a) there is known unmet need and therefore little possibility of TSN's being used against caravans because they (caravans) cannot be relocated to a suitable site elsewhere in the area) (b) in areas where LPA's are known to be unwilling to use TSN's or lack effective enforcement resources – perhaps due to fiscal austerity

6/ Does the Government anticipate that TSN's would be used by LPA's at established sites where 'overspill' is occurring (i.e. where larger than permitted numbers are in evidence at an established site) OR where named (permitted) occupants have moved on (e.g. in the scenario of a 'named temporary permission occupier') and new occupants have moved onto the site (possibly having bought the pitch from the former owner)? Clearly 'overspill' and unlawful 'succession' are in essence unlawful occupations and the Government need to be clear at the use and consequence of new TSN's in these situations

7/ What are the penalties for non compliance with a TSN? e.g. where a caravan occupant refuses to relocate to a unauthorised site. And is the occupant able to refuse to relocate on the grounds that an alternative site is shared by a different 'type' of traveller (e.g. Irish travellers/Romany Gypsies/ New Age travellers) with whom s/he shares cultural differences

8/ Are static and mobile homes (e.g. 'Park Homes') classified as caravans or buildings for the purposes of The Town and Country Planning Act 1990 and for the purposes of the proposed TSN's. If an unlawful development involved the use of such dwellings would the LPA be able to serve a TSN against such a structure if it was a 'main residence'?

9/ What is mean specifically by *'the availability of alternative traveller* sites'. Is this the 5 year deliverable supply of sites mentioned in the previous guidance 'Planning Policy for Traveller Sites' or would it simply relate to pitches which are available locally to accommodate caravans which have been moved as a result of the TSN being served upon them? Clarification is required given that the availability of other traveller sites will be a determining factor as to whether to serve a TSN. If it is the case that a Local authority does not have, at a particular point in time, an up to date 5 year supply of traveller sites, does it follow therefore that it will be deprived of a tool to prevent unauthorised developments involving the stationing of caravans?

10/ Will legal aid be available to challenge TSN's at Judicial Review? The availability (or lack of it) may be a significant factor in the number of judicial challenges.

SECTION THREE

Potential Policies

From discussions with groups from the settled community affected by unauthorised developments (including a number of local Councillors) –the following policy suggestions have been made:

Policy suggestion no.1

'Empower the Local Authorities' Overview and Scrutiny functions to review Councils' current attainments and engender new holistic policies to promote identification and fulfilment of Gypsy and Traveller Accommodation need'

The Overview and Scrutiny function of Local Authorities has a crucial role in holding Executive members to account for decisions taken. It has a specific role in policy-development. These functions were conferred on Councils by the Local Government Act 2000. This Overview and Scrutiny role has a wide-ranging remit to link up with partners, consult with residents and produce new local policy.

This policy paper suggests that specific legislative provision should be made to require Local Councils – via their scrutiny functions - to

- Verify whether the authority has policies and plans in place to identify and meet unmet gypsy and traveller needs

- Launch an investigation as to which specific policy gaps exist and, where necessary, create a 'Task Group' charged with filling these gaps in a timely manner by enlisting the support of multiagency partners

- Carry out such investigations as may be needed TO IDENTIFY potential locations of new Gypsy and Traveller sites where there is robust evidence of need or intelligence indicating such need

- Launch local consultation to publicise evidence-based need for new sites – and find potential local solutions

Overview and scrutiny can be a highly focused improvement planning function within any local authority. We suggest that it be given new powers to find solutions to Gypsy and Traveller needs which will encompass a range of pertinent issues and agencies (Housing, Highways, Education, Planning, Health) etc.

Equality in Planning

It should be THE repository for cross-party and multi-agency working to plan for traveller sites in partnership with the settled community. It should be THE focus for action by Local Authorities who find themselves lagging behind in their statutory commitments.

A new focus for Gypsy and Traveller planning through scrutiny will enable the Local Authority to 'kick start' the process of engagement with the community.

The settled community will have the opportunity to engage – early - in discussions regarding the need for site provision which may affect their community and environment (with a reduced threat of the arbitrary imposition of 'temporary' permissions) in the same way that developers building 'bricks and mortar' accommodation have to address issues such as social cohesion and environmental sustainability on a joint basis.

For public and private sites, the travelling community will also have the opportunity to:

- Make their case for accommodation - free from the tensions and conflict which almost always accompany 'forced' or unauthorised developments

- Work with the settled community, planners and politicians to address suitable provision on a 'plan led' basis

- Focus more of their scarce resources on achievable developments at appropriately located private sites rather than pay considerable expenses at appeal e.g. for Barristers, Planning Consultants, expert witnesses and the like

- Achieve peaceful co-existence – rather than fight local resentment from the settled community emanating from what appears to be 'forced' permissions which reflect arbitrary targets

- Engage with the community to plan for sites which have better access to local services

Equality in Planning

Policy suggestion no.2

'It should be a Criminal Offence to launch residential and commercial developments without Planning Permission – with a statutory defence of genuine mistake. This aims to outlaw the use of retrospective planning applications by developers who seek to use this as a device to launch residential and commercial development and use legal sanctions to enforce 'plan-led' development in the countryside'

We propose that unlawful development should in fact be a criminal offence. This will constrain all landowners, tenants and others from damaging green belt, agricultural areas, areas of outstanding natural beauty or local wildlife sites with intent to secure retrospective planning permission to construct multiple residential premises or construct/carry out commercial development.

It is not currently a criminal offence to develop land without planning permission. An offence arises only if an enforcement notice is not complied with. The penalties on conviction are a fine of up to £20,000 in the magistrates' court or an unlimited fine on indictment. The local planning authority can also enter the land and do what is necessary to enforce judgement and recover expenses from the landowner.

The official Government view was expressed via The Department for Communities and Local Government in February 2012:

The issue of making a breach of planning control a punishable offence has been considered before, first by Parliament in the debates culminating in the Planning and Compensation Act 1991, and again following a consultation on a review of planning enforcement in 2006. On both occasions the view was taken that criminalisation would be an inappropriate and disproportionate response, and would also impose additional burdens on hard pressed Magistrates Courts.

However, the Government does take unauthorised development very seriously. Whilst there are no plans to criminalise planning breaches of a particular type, the enforcement measures that have been included in the Localism Act will enhance the existing powers available to local planning authorities. Given the range of powers that are and will become available, it is considered that effective enforcement of all planning breaches can be maintained provided the powers are used correctly and promptly.

Equality in Planning

This response, however, does not take account of

- The potential and probable deterrent effect on unauthorised developers, prompting them to seek plan led solutions first rather than act first and defend later (thereby supporting the case for prior discussion, consultation and negotiation before submitting plans)

- The subsequent reductions in legal fees and costs to the taxpayers incurred in taking lengthy legal action to seek redress (and then enforcement) following unauthorised development

- The undermining effect on community cohesion caused by unlawful developments and the deleterious effect of the actions of a few on the reputation of Gypsies and Travellers as a whole

- The benefits of the restoration of a public sense of fairness in disincentivising equally and across the board all unlawful development

We contend therefore that it IS proportionate' to make unlawful development a punishable – and expensive – offence.

Protesters gather in Eaves Green Lane

Just to cite a few recent cases which have done serious damage at once to the countryside and to the reputation of Travellers and Gypsies:

Case study: Eaves Green Lane, Meriden, West Midlands. A Bank holiday development which destroyed acres of land and carried out unlawful business activities on an agricultural unit and adjoining land also owned by the developers. A retrospective application was made for a residential Gypsy site for fourteen pitches, each comprising a mobile home, touring caravan, and utility building, plus grassed amenity area and parking/turning area.

Equality in Planning

Case study: Kites Nest Lane, Beausale, Warwickshire. This site is 11 miles from the Meriden site. An unlawful development occurred during the Bank Holiday at precisely the same time as the Meriden site. A retrospective application was made for the change of use of the site for British Romany Gypsy families for thirteen permanent pitches for mobile homes, thirteen touring caravans for nomadic use only and thirteen utility day rooms and also authorised the serving of an Enforcement Notice.

Case study: Hardhorn, Poulton-le-fylde, Lancashire. Unlawful development work starts under cover of darkness and, despite 'Stop' Notice and an injunction, continues. This leads locals to conclude that 'Current legal and planning remedies do not work'. It is argued that straightforward criminalisation of land desecration would allow direct intervention by the Police to halt activities.

Case study: Barnacle near Rugby. The occupants moved onto the site without benefit of planning permission on the evening of Friday 24th September 2010. A Temporary 'Stop' Notice was issued on Friday 24th September 2010 and the provisions of this notice have been effectively continued by the High Court, who, following an application from the Council, made an injunction order. A retrospective application was made to change the use of land for use as a residential caravan site for gypsy families, comprising three pitches and the siting of three mobile homes and a further three touring caravans including ancillary works (part retrospective).

Case study: Land on the north-east Side of Southend Lane, Newent Gloucestershire. Unlawful and unauthorised development occurred at the beginning of the Whitsun holiday in 2009. Residents suddenly became aware at approximately 5 PM in the evening that lorries laden with hard-core were travelling down the lane. Initially, it was thought that a farmer was filling in potholes in an access road, but lorry activity rapidly increased. Shocked by the scale of the activity, local residents were initially unable to respond. The local authority could not be contacted because of the holiday. By the end of the weekend some 70 lorries had delivered gravel and hard core substantially covering one half of the field; caravans were moved onto the site and by the end of the weekend the local authority was faced by a *fait accompli*.

A retrospective application for Change of Use of land for the stationing of thirteen Gypsy caravan pitches with provision of utility/day room buildings, propane gas tanks, hard standings, access road, landscaping, fencing and drainage facilities all ancillary to that use was subsequently submitted.

Equality in Planning

Case study: Land lying to the east of The Causeway, Clophill, Bedfordshire MK45 4BA.
Caravans moved onto the site during Easter bank holiday of April 4th 2010. The plot had previously been sold and in November 2009 was cleared of all shrubbery and then fenced off. Tarmac and gravel were imported and laid. This shows a clear and pre-meditated intent to develop by stealth as distinct from a plan-led development. A retrospective Planning Application was made for the siting of

one static caravan, one touring caravan, and parking for two vehicles.

Case study: Theale, Somerset. Two gypsy families turned a 1.7 acre greenfield paddock which they owned into an 'urban development' on Good Friday 2009, by laying tons of hard-core and constructing fencing around several caravans. A retrospective Planning Application followed.

Case study: Dale Farm. Dale Farm. is a six acre plot of land, including the site of a former scrap yard, in the village of Cray's Hill. Since 2001, travellers have breached planning law by setting up homes in caravans, developing hard standings and road access across the site. There were 51 illegal pitches involving up to 240 people on the site. Next to the illegal Dale Farm site there is also an **authorised** travellers' site known as Oak Lane, which is legal and which gained planning permission between 1992 and 1996. The Oak Lane site provides 34 legal pitches.

In July 2011, Basildon Council issued a 28 day notice to travellers occupying the unauthorised pitches on the site known as Dale Farm, requiring them to vacate the land in accordance with enforcement notices served over many previous years. Eviction ensued later that year.

Equality in Planning

Policy suggestion no.3

Local Authorities should be able to impose a range of penalties on developers who create unauthorised developments 'on the back of previously permitted developments'. These, though their imposition and extent must be guided by considerations of proportionality, could include:

- *Automatic fines for developers who abuse the opportunity afforded by <u>authorised permissions</u> (e.g. to provide services to a site) to launch a subsequent, unauthorised residential development, retrospectively applying for Planning Permission*

- *Possibility of revocation of original Planning Applications for subsequent abuse.*

- *Application of Stop Notices/Injunctions to the site*

Background: A lawful Planning approval (uncontested by reasonable neighbours) should surely be welcomed and those neighbours' goodwill and readiness to adapt reciprocated.

Alas, it has frequently been rewarded only by abuse. A successful application for development of a modest site is seen as precedent for a much larger, undeclared development which is launched unlawfully – usually while plant and equipment is on site carrying out the authorised work. Such abuses are amongst the principal reasons for public mistrust of the travelling community and for shortage of available sites. Perpetrators are phenomenally misguided and short-sighted, and Travellers no less than the settled should welcome measures which will prevent further instances.

In almost every instance thus far recorded, decision makers would never have approved the initial work had it been known to be part of a larger development, but are now presented with a fait accompli. Intensive and rapid enforcement action (*Stop" Notice, Injunction) is needed to check the unauthorised work, but too often the momentum is with the developer who completes much of the work before any action can be taken. Again, the work is often timed to co-coincide with Bank Holidays when Planning enforcement officers are not available.

Equality in Planning

Case study: Hady Lane Chesterfield. Travellers arrived a couple of days before Christmas on open countryside land which they had purchased. Their approved planning application (uncontested by neighbours) was for the construction of paddocks and wooden storage sheds, which allowed them to prepare the site under this cover. They then moved in three caravans and created new hard standing and parking areas. A traveller site application for two mobile homes/ traveller sites was submitted retrospectively.

Case study: Hardhorn, Poulton-le-fylde, Lancashire. Stop notices and threats of injunction did not serve as a deterrent to ongoing unauthorised work.

Policy suggestion no. 4

Stricter enforcement penalties for 'additional activities and blights' on land owned by developers which can accompany unauthorised developments'

Unauthorised developments are often accompanied by other activities which damage the land and quality of life of visitors and local residents and businesses. These include *tipping / rubbish dumping and stockpiling, cable burning and parking of scrap cars & caravans etc. as they are acts that are alien to normal acceptable activities in green belt / green barrier land.*

It seems reasonable that all those seeking approval to develop a site should submit a thorough assessment of all environmental effects, and, as a condition of that approval, sign an undertaking that they will conduct themselves responsibly, courteously and with respect for their neighbours and their environment. Any failure to abide by this undertaking should be penalised and potentially render void rights of tenure. Environmental effects in excess of those foreseen in the assessment should at once be made good at the developer's expense. Such a contract is implicit in any tenancy or land-ownership, but Noah Burton, the leader of the Meriden gypsies, is content that it be explicit in cases such as his.

"We are two dogs with one bone," he told us, "and we are very much the smaller and the hungrier dog, so concessions are in order. We are peaceable and law-abiding. You can check the police records and the planning records. There have been no complaints since we arrived. Of course we cannot be held accountable for every member of our community all the time, though I'll warrant we're closer and tougher disciplinarians than many settled families, but we're happy to undertake, as a community, to do nothing offensive or illegal and are content that that should be a condition of approval."

Equality in Planning

Media coverage and generalisations may have been unjust, but the travelling community must nonetheless confront and overcome their effects. Again and again, responsible travellers have declared to us their willingness to be bound by such undertakings, conditional for a probationary period following occupation. This would do much to enhance public tolerance of the travelling community and to assist integration.

For those developers, travelling or settled, unwilling to make such a commitment, stricter penalties for disregard for the environment should be available and should be imposed.

This is not and must never be victimisation of one section of society. It is recognised throughout society that the environment is threatened and in urgent need of protection. That starts in our own backyards. The consequences of wilful disregard for the environment may be grave or even irrevocable. This gravity should be reflected in the conditions of planning approval and in the penalties meted out to those, settled or travelling, private or commercial, who violate our most precious resource.

Case Study: Meriden (see above) Travellers used their adjacent premises to dump unwanted tarmac and other building waste. The material emanated from paving work carried out in the nearby village.

Policy suggestion no.5

Specify the limits and scale of a retrospective planning application to ensure that it is not used as a device to force residential or commercial development.

Any Planning system needs an element of 'retrospectivity' to ensure that honest mistakes and other errors can be lawfully assessed. Developers are however using the retrospective provision to 'steal a march' on the Planning system and evade pre-development scrutiny. This is a denial of the 'plan led' philosophy underpinning any fair planning system. It also denies or 'robs' citizens, neighbours and other interested parties of the opportunity to comment/object/support developments before commencement or completion of the project.

Equality in Planning

We suggest that retrospective applications for multiple residential properties or commercial enterprises be automatically refused pending full examination of the case and the completion of due process. We suggest that more indicative guidelines be produced by Councils to spell out the scope of retrospective developments (e.g. individual windows)

The Government feels that it is already dealing in part with retrospective developments through the Localism Act.

'One step already taken is a provision in the new Localism Act to limit retrospective planning applications for unauthorised development. The provision will allow either appeal against enforcement action or a retrospective planning application, but not both. This is designed to crack down on the unscrupulous who 'play the system' by drawing out the period for appealing against enforcement action by also submitting a retrospective application for planning permission, thus enabling unauthorised development to remain. It is our intention to close off that option by early April.

It should be noted however that this does not deal with the classic 'Bank Holiday Blitz' scenario where a developer carries out an unlawful activity whilst simultaneously lodging a planning application. The developer is very often determined to follow the appeal route to the 'nth' degree and does not necessarily use the device described above. So this policy development initiative is 'off target' when it comes to the main issue of methods to deal with retrospective applications.

Our policy suggestion is straightforward – only small scale 'overlooked' issues in development qualify for retrospective approval. The use of retrospective application to 'steal a march on the planning system' for residential and commercial development should be outlawed.

Equality in Planning

Policy suggestion no.6

'When unauthorised developers, local residents and the Council 'lock horns' in Planning disputes, they can go on for years fuelled by 'appeal upon appeal' costing both sides huge amounts of money (or the taxpayer where appeals are supported by legal aid) AND generating uncertainty'.

We suggest that such disputes (often fuelled by countless appeals and planning applications - often aimed at prolonging occupation time at unlawful sites) should be subjected to a **'limitation order'**. This order would fix the period of dispute for a maximum of two years – including appeal decisions.

Case study: Meriden. Bank holiday development destroyed acres of land and also carried out unlawful business activities on an agricultural unit on adjoining land also owned by the developers.

The Gypsies at the Meriden site signed a voluntary agreement to leave (in March 2012) following defeat of their High Court Appeal (288a) in exchange for a years' grace to find an alternative site. Despite this pledge to leave, the Gypsies launched a fresh planning application (refused) for an injuncted adjoining site and also launched a fresh appeal to overturn the 288a Decision through the Court of Appeal. These actions fuel the impression amongst residents that (a) 'there is virtually no end to the appeal process' (b) pledges provided by the Gypsies are simply given to 'buy time' until the next appeal and (c) any dispute involving travellers takes years to resolve underlining the statement made by the Secretary of State that 'justice delayed is justice denied'

Case study: Southend Lane Newent. Following the appeal hearing in December 2009, some six months after the initial unlawful development, the appeal was dismissed but a temporary permission of two years allowed in order to prepare to quit the site which needed to be returned to its original state. An enforcement order was also applied to the remainder of the field to ensure no further extension of illegal development.

Equality in Planning

During 2011 it was clear that not all of the thirteen placements which have been created on the site were in use, suggesting that demand by travellers was comparatively limited. A close watch was kept on the site as the date for vacating the site came closer (end of January 2012). There was no indication that travellers were either seeking alternative accommodation themselves or were preparing to move. Indeed the day before the local authority was due to check the site to see what had happened on February 1, several caravans were moved onto the site. The day after the local authority visit, they were again removed.

Another planning proposal had been submitted to the local authority in October 2011. This was rapidly rejected. As was anticipated, in the last weeks of January, a <u>further</u> new planning proposal was submitted, this one more substantially structured than the previous one although substantial elements of the submission remained exactly the same as those put in two years before.

Local residents who opposed the scheme were outraged to discover that the new planning permission had to be dealt with as entirely separate from anything which had happened before - almost as though the site itself was virgin land.... although, of course, in this instance it should be treated as agricultural. The local authority, to date, has received large numbers of complaints from local people as has the town council. The most recent move by the local authority – indeed, before a decision on the planning submission has been taken – has been the issuing of a further enforcement notice giving the travellers six months' notice to quit.

Coalition policy has attempted to mitigate the 'appeal on appeal' phenomena and can be summarised as follows:

'One step already taken is a provision in the new Localism Act to limit retrospective planning applications for unauthorised development. The provision will allow either appeal against enforcement action or a retrospective planning application, but not both. This is designed to crack down on the unscrupulous who 'play the system' by drawing out the period for appealing against enforcement action by also submitting a retrospective application for planning permission, thus enabling unauthorised development to remain. It is our intention to close off that option by early April' DCLG correspondence.

This provision, however would not deal with retrospective applications or multiple planning applications to the same site.

Equality in Planning

Policy suggestion no.7

'Use the 'duty to co-operate' enshrined in the Localism Act to co-ordinate action against unlawful developments which have taken place simultaneously in neighbouring and nearby Authorities to save time and reduce costs to taxpayers'

Where a development occurs to a virtually simultaneous timescale in neighbouring vicinities it makes sense for adjoining Authorities to co-ordinate action to reduce enforcement and other legal costs.

Case study: Simultaneous unauthorised developments occurred in at **Hardhorn** and **Preesall.** Although only a few miles apart, the sites are situated in two different Borough Councils. The HSSP site is within the boundary of Fylde Borough Council (FBC). The Preesall site is within the Wyre Borough Council (WBC) boundary. The two sets of travellers are related and, initially, made a joint planning application.

Case study: Meriden and **Beausale.** These sites are approximately 11 miles apart. Occupation took place on the same day and employed the services of the same external consultants and expert witnesses (for the appellants) and the same legal Counsel for the Local Authorities. Protesters from the settled community also used the same legal Counsel. The question should be asked 'what economies of scale could exist in fees, logistics and planning matters to deal with both issues as a 'job lot' whilst recognising the particular differences inherent in each case (e.g. family circumstances, local ecology)

An associated issue relates to whether the 'duty to co-operate' in the Localism Act coiuld have wider implications across UK and Irish boundaries to promote information sharing to validate or counter occupancy related claims made by travellers involved in planning disputes. This could 'weed out' developers who simultaneously launch different unlawful developments at different locations or valid the nomadic or displaced occupancy claims of travellers.

Equality in Planning

Policy suggestion no.8

'Only allow one appeal following a decision by the Planning Inspectorate to prevent the glacial timescales involved in resolving disputes'

We believe that unauthorised developments have been set up with the deliberate intention to 'steal a march' on the planning process. It is also widely recognised that unlawful developers deliberately employ an 'appeal-on-appeal' strategy in hope of gaining up to a decade of occupancy. Contrived attempts to manipulate the planning system should result in a degree of forfeiture in the subsequent appeals process.

This 'Dale Farm Syndrome' wastes travellers' and taxpayers' money and the time of Local Authorities and the Courts alike. Disputes should be settled more quickly and a limitation set on the number of appeals. The leader of Basildon Council noted recently.

"I was however and remain annoyed that £1.6 million was added to our final bill by the delay and legal costs incurred between September and October when the travellers launched their last minute legal challenge against the Council's right to clear Dale Farm."

We therefore propose that the nature of, and all grounds for, an appeal should be established from the outset and that further appeals and applications relating to the same property/properties or divers uses cannot subsequently be made if the initial appeal be unsuccessful (unless substantive additional evidence, unavailable to the appellant at the time of the initial application, can be adduced).

Case study: Hardhorn, Poulton-le-fylde, Lancashire et al. Multiple appeals serve only to 'string out' action against unlawful sites and 'wear down' local opposition.

Case study: Theale Somerset: Following a 'Good Friday 2009' bank holiday development, an enforcement notice was issued by Sedgemoor District council on 17th April 2009.

The retrospective application for planning permission was refused by the planning officer on 26th May. Residents unaware of the 'glacial' pace involved in such matters were shocked by the timescales involved in addressing these issues. An appeal by the developers was heard on 24 and 25 November 2009. The appeal was refused on 11th January 2010 and a date set for the travellers to move by the 11th July 2010.

Equality in Planning

Following a further application (High Court, 8th March 2012) for "leave to appeal against the inspector's decision" which was refused, a further planning application was lodged for the land. The council had been intending to seek an injunction to remove them, but were advised they had to consider the new application, even though it was very similar to the first one. This was refused in August 2011. A further appeal has now been lodged with no date set for that appeal. An application for legal aid is understood to have been made to continue the appeal process.

Local residents are 'very frustrated' at the length of time and cost involved can see no end in sight to the appeal-upon-appeal strategy being deployed.

Policy suggestion no.9

'Gypsy and Traveller need should more robustly be identified and addressed to prevent unlawful developers using 'target figures' as a rationale for launching unlawful developments'

It is undoubtedly the case that some developers who are planning an unauthorised development look to Planning consultants and other advisers to (a) research the level of assessed 'unmet need' in a given Local Planning Authority area and then (b) shape their development application so that it closely – or exactly – matches assessed levels of unmet need.

The consequences of this are that:

- Many people feel that that the planning system is being cynically manipulated by developers. 'How much can I get away with?' as distinct from 'What need is there?' is widely perceived as the question behind applications.

- Unmet need allocation is 'used up' by unlawful developers and may cause other, more deserving planning applications (e.g. at authorised sites who wish to expand to accommodate family growth) to be rejected.

- Individual gypsies and travellers contribute to the negative perception of the travelling community when on the one hand they claim that their unlawful developments were provoked by a family crisis yet, on the other, the developments correspond closely or exactly to the 'level of unmet need' in the area.

Equality in Planning

Case study: Hardhorn and Preesall. (separate) sites. The number of pitches established at both sites in Nov 2009 tallies exactly with the number required by the Regional Spatial Strategy.

Case study: Southend Lane, Newent. During 2011, it was clear that not all of the thirteen pitches created on the site were in use, suggesting that demand from travellers was comparatively limited. A close watch was kept on the site as the date for vacating the site came closer (end of January 2012). There was no indication that travellers were either seeking alternative accommodation themselves or were preparing to move. Indeed, the day before the local authority was due to check the site to see what had happened on February 1, several caravans were moved onto the site. The day after the local authority visit, they were again removed.

Case study: Meriden. The original retrospective application was made for fourteen pitches which were then reduced to ten. A further application to reduce the pitch numbers to eight has since been made at appeal. This clearly suggests that developers are attempting to 'feel their way' toward an acceptable number as distinct from producing clear evidence of verifiable need. Anecdotal information suggest that the site has been unoccupied – save by a caretaker - during the evening for over a year.

Policy suggestion no.10

'Withdraw legal aid for land owners contesting unauthorised development planning decisions'

We suggest that where unauthorised developments have been set up with the manifest intention of 'stealing a march' on the planning process, this should not be supported through the provision of Legal Aid. It is also recognised that unlawful developers deliberately factor in an 'appeal on appeal on appeal' into their strategy in the hope to gaining a decade of occupancy in the hope of ultimately gaining approval. This long distance 'permission through attrition' approach should not be funded by taxpayers.

Case Study: Dale Farm. This has highlighted the large sums of money provided in legal aid over a decade and through the recent pre-eviction period.

Equality in Planning

The most pertinent provision relating to this is the Legal Aid Bill[1] which was published on the 21st June 2011 and seeks to address in part how Legal Aid provision should be determined for Gypsies and Travellers in housing related appeals.

'The main types of Gypsy and Traveller cases that require public funding are those which concern: evictions from unauthorised encampments; evictions from rented sites; other issues relating to rented sites; high court and county court planning cases (injunctions, planning appeals, challenges to stop notices and direct action etc); and homelessness cases'.
Community Law Partnership

The key issue currently being debated is what is 'in scope' and WILL receive legal aid funding and what is not. We suggest that Legal Aid provision should NOT be extended to Judicial Review in appeal cases relating to unauthorised developments using retrospective mechanisms in an attempt to force development.

An alternative to this approach would be to provide a review legal aid provision in vexatious cases which ran parallel to the appeal process so prevent further delays in specific cases.

[1] *Legal Aid, Sentencing and Punishment of Offenders Bill 2011*

Policy suggestion no.11

For the purpose of planning applications to develop land, there should be a duty of proof to prove a current or previous nomadic lifestyle where it is alleged that there is a land requirement emanating from that need.

Where developers claim that they should be categorised as Gypsies or Travellers for the purpose of Planning Applications, there should a duty of proof of this claim.

It would be for the Local Authority to establish what would constitute reliable and robust evidence in this matter.

Policy suggestion no.12

'In very special circumstances Local Authorities should be allowed to 'opt out' of making any or more provision for Gypsies and Travellers in the short to medium term. Special dispensation shall be sought from the Secretary of State outlining the reasons for which exemption is sought. Authorities shall give a timescale for the exemption period to apply and may – at any point – revisit the issue of provision'

There may be areas of where it is currently impossible to make provision for Gypsies and Travellers and this may be further reinforced by data which suggests that there is no discernible need. In such circumstances letters of exemption would be sought by the relevant Authority.

This would not exempt a Local Authority from carrying out a review to ascertain whether such need has changed.

Case Study: The City of Westminster Council LDP. (adopted Sept 2011) states:

'No sites have been allocated for Gypsy and Traveller pitches, reflecting the densely built up nature of the city and scarcity of vacant land. Temporary sites may become available as part of the redevelopment process. The policy provides the criteria for assessing any proposals for pitches. The protection of residential amenity and townscape is vitally important in Westminster due to its dense historic urban fabric…'

Policy suggestion no.13

'Provide the Local Authority with powers to quash prior planning permissions where it is proven that a permitted use is not being adhered and/or where locations are the focus of human rights violations – e.g. so called 'slave sites'

This policy would relate to any premises where (a) there has been proven and systematic abuse of occupants on a site (e.g. prostitution, 'slave sites' etc. and (b) where the Local Authority determine that the revocation of existing permissions would form part of a wider package of measures to prevent the issue reoccurring.

Local Authorities would also need to take into account the effects of such revocation on (a) others that were deemed innocent of any involvement (but were dependent on the location/ site) and (b) the likely impact on others who may benefit from the site in future (e.g. new occupants)

Case study: Green Acres Caravan Park in Leighton Buzzard, Beds.

Equality in Planning

Policy suggestion no.14

'There should be a 'duty to co-operate' placed upon <u>utility service providers</u> to consult with Local Authorities as to whether planning permission has been obtained prior to the installation of NEW services at previously UNDEVELOPED locations'

Unlawful developments may be preceded by applications to service providers to connect services. Where new services are requested (e.g. first time supply), the utility company would have placed upon it a 'duty of care' to ensure that the land carries with it the relevant planning permissions.

This is seen as:

- A potential deterrent to unlawful developers
- A 'early warning' opportunity for Local Authorities and
- A means of building and maintaining the reputation of utility suppliers e.g. not all business is good business and suppliers should not wish to be seen to be complicit with unlawful development

Utility companies and others (e.g. Building materials suppliers) may wish to regard this as part of their 'Corporate Social Responsibility' commitment - to act in a way which avoids fuelling community tension and conflict.

Policy suggestion no.15

There should be a 'duty of care' placed upon <u>Local Authorities</u> to consult with their own internal Departments and suppliers to guard against potential unlawful developments – particularly at UNDEVELOPED locations.

Unlawful developers can – deliberately or unwittingly – take advantage of a Local Authority's poor internal communications. Departmental working should be 'joined up' and underpinned with a 'Duty of Care' – particularly in relevant Departments such as Planning, Licensing, Building Regulations and Legal Services.

This duty of care – when underpinned with a streamlined process would be seen to be:

- A potential deterrent to unlawful developers
- A 'early warning' opportunity for Local Authorities and
- A means of building and maintaining the reputation of the Local Authority

Local Authorities may wish to regard this as part of their 'Corporate Social Responsibility' commitment (underpinned by a constitutional commitment) to act in a way which avoids fuelling community tension and conflict.

Equality in Planning

Policy suggestion 16

'Outlaw 'ransom sales' of land to the public by developers and owners who seek inflated returns on land values where sites have been – or maybe - at the centre of conflict and tension'

Unlawful developers should not be able to profit from the misery of the settled community by offering land back for sale to the community which has been at the centre of a community dispute. Trading Standards or another relevant body should have a role in mediating and – where necessary – warning owners, land agents and estate agents of over-inflated values.

It is also clear from anecdotal evidence that landowners from the settled community have sought to inflate land values by using the threat of selling land to travellers to 'incentivise' the local market to buy the land.

Case study: Meriden. Three acres of land at the centre of a planning dispute has been advertised as 'for sale by auction' for a price of '£150,000 to £200,000'. The land has formed part of a larger plot owned by Gypsies. A realistic local market valuation is £15,000 - £20,000 for the 3 acre site. The owner is seeking some 10 times the market valuation (http://www.loveitts.co.uk/land/sales/meriden/eaves-green-lane).

It is known anecdotally that some community groups have paid 'ransom' prices to simply 'buy off' an unlawful developer – using their own pension fund money and life savings to acquire land which they neither need or desire. Purchasers are embarrassed at buying land at inflated prices, do not wish to court publicity and cite – as their reasons for purchasing the site – their desire to move unlawful developers on and protect the site for the future. In these circumstances unlawful developers feel that they are in a 'no lose' situation. If their (usually retrospective) planning application / appeals are successful, they have added considerable value to a site – and if they lose they can offer the land for re-sale at inflated prices.

If this was viewed as 'interference in the free market', conditions could be placed on such sites by Planning Authorities to remove permitted development rights on contentious sites (Article 4 Direction). A developer could seek to have this rescinded upon purchase if they could demonstrate (via a Planning Application) that any future specified use would be (a) appropriate to the site and (b) not harm the associated amenities of – and surrounding – the site e.g. impact on character and openness, highway safety and so on.

Equality in Planning

Policy suggestion 17

'Support proposed changes to Temporary Stop Notices to ensure that unlawful developments AND unlawful occupations cease at the same time until the outcome of any (retrospective) Planning Application and subsequent Appeals are known'

As has been demonstrated, although Temporary Stop Notices (and the use of other devices such as Injunctions) serve to 'freeze' development they do not address the issue of ongoing unlawful occupation. Gypsies and Travellers continue to enjoy the benefit of occupation of land unlawfully for many years pending the outcome of extended appeals. Changes to Temporary Stop Notices to prevent occupation would render the 'business case' for unlawful developments untenable as they would have to cease AND withdraw from a site within a short period of occupation (e.g. within a few months)

The Government has already stated that:

Councils would be given greater freedom to stop unauthorised traveller sites being set up and prevent long, drawn-out stalemates like Dale Farm, under proposals announced by Communities Secretary Eric Pickles.

The proposals would allow councils greater freedom to choose when to use 'Temporary Stop Notices' in relation to caravans which are used as main residences and are in breach of planning control. This would be backed up with the potential for heavy fines.

Temporary Stop Notices enable councils to take immediate action against unauthorised development without having to wait three days for a Stop Notice, or 28 for an Enforcement Notice to come into effect (by which time it becomes costly and much more difficult to enforce against).

Under the current system councils are constrained as to when they can use these powers against caravans which are main residences. A small minority has sought to abuse the planning system, and the Government believes that this proposal will assist local councils in taking effective action. It is the Government's view that local councils are best placed to judge whether to use a Temporary Stop Notice in relation to caravans, and should not be constrained by blanket rules.

Subject to the outcome of consultation, the proposals would remove restrictions on the use of Temporary Stop Notices and help councils to act immediately and safeguard their local area from the emergence of unauthorised sites.

This would provide a strong deterrent, and any person guilty of this offence is liable to a fine of up to £20,000, which can be increased to an unlimited fine, on conviction on indictment in the Crown Court.

...licy suggestion is welcome and advice is sought as to how this would be ...npatible with (a) Human Rights Legislation (b) Planning Policy for Traveller Sites policy Ministerial Guidance and (c) Local Authority determinations which still may be made prior to the vacation of a site (in its consideration of whether site occupation, general unmet need and other traveller specific information) would yet still constitute 'very special circumstances to overcome both the provisions of an amended Temporary Stop Notice and the 'very special circumstances cited by travellers to overcome greenbelt (et al) protections. A series of related questions – seeking clarification of the operation and effect of the TSN's are outlined in section 2 above.